W9-DCM-782

[CONTENTS]

© 2003 American Library Association.
Adapted from Poetry Slam, Inc., www.poetryslam.com.
By Michael Baldwin. Used by permission.
ISBN 0-8389-4037-4
Printed in the United States of America

[PREFACE]

This manual is designed to help you produce and participate in a poetry slam program. It will also provide techniques for successful slam performances. The manual is primarily directed to young people who are interested in becoming performance poets and participating in slams, but it should be helpful to anyone interested in poetry slams and their production.

The rules provided in this manual are based on those of Poetry Slam, Inc., the national slam poetry organization that sanctions local slams for the official national competition. However, I have taken the liberty of abbreviating some of the rules for greater clarity, and I have also included some generally accepted practices that are assumed but not specifically addressed in the official rules. I wish to express appreciation for the particular assistance and cooperation received from Steve Marsh, executive director of Poetry Slam, Inc.

—*Michael Baldwin*

[INTRODUCTION]

Poetry competitions have been around since ancient times. In those days, when most people didn't read and write, it was the poet who was the memory of the community. He took the great stories of the tribe and made poems of them. He put them into rhyme and meter to more easily memorize them. Then he recited them for the entertainment and enlightenment of the populace. When several poets got together, they taught each other poems and had festivals of poetry. Sometimes these became competitions to decide who could present poems most effectively.

As oral traditions waned, and writing could be used to record history and legend, poets were still revered for the entertainment, wisdom, and ceremonial authority they provided. Poetic forms proliferated, and poetry was practiced primarily as an art form.

Today we still need public poetry when emotionally charged moments require our best words. It is poetry that can best express our greatest wisdom, our most intense emotions, our most sublime ideas.

[WHAT IS A POETRY SLAM?]

The ancient tradition of poetry competition was revived and updated in the 1980s in Chicago, when a former construction worker named Marc Smith began to hold poetry competitions in a local bar. He called them slams to emphasize the competitive aspect of these emotionally charged poetic outpourings. They quickly became so popular that a formal set of rules had to be created to keep the competitions manageable and to determine winners in a fair manner.

Today, you can find poetry slams in any large city and many smaller ones. Poets often compete to become part of a city's official slam team and thereby compete in regional, state, and national competitions.

The main thing about poetry slams is they are just great fun for all concerned. They provide high energy, intense emotion, the thrill of victory, and the agony of defeat. Slams encourage people to write poetry and to appreciate the art and performance of poetic expression. Slam poetry provides a creative outlet for the exuberant emotion and questing intellect of young people especially.

WHAT IS NEEDED TO PRODUCE A POETRY SLAM?

The basic ingredients of a poetry slam are the following:

1. **A slam venue.** This is the place where you hold the slam. Any large room that will comfortably hold a seated audience and allow them to see and hear the performer will do. A well-lighted stage or podium for the performer and a microphone sound system are helpful, but not essential. The venue should allow for a lot of noise, since the crowd is encouraged to be enthusiastic in their response to the competition.

2. **An emcee** (master of ceremonies). Often known as the "SlamMaster," the emcee:
   - presides over the competition to keep it under control, moving forward, and to make sure everyone keeps to the rules;
   - selects the judges from the audience and instructs them and the audience in the process of judging;
   - supervises setting the performance order, which will be determined by an audience member drawing names from a container;

- announces the name of each competitor when it is time for him or her to perform; and
- asks the judges to hold up their score cards a few seconds after each performance and announces each score. The emcee then announces the composite score (as computed by the score keeper).

The emcee must make sure to act completely impartially toward all the competitors so as not to bias the judges in any way. The emcee should probably only address the audience and not the performers. He or she should encourage the audience to applaud each performer.

3. **Judges.** These are usually selected from the audience by the emcee. The judges must be impartial toward the competitors. It's best that they don't even know the competitors. There should be at least three judges, and preferably five. They don't need to know anything about poetry. The main requirements of good judges are that they can produce a score quickly after each performance and that they are consistent in the way they score. Judges should give equal weight to the poem's content and the poet's performance. The judges should also resist being influenced by the audience reaction to the performances. See the Judging and Scoring Rules on page 13 for details.

4. **Score cards.** Each judge should be given two sets of score cards. These can be made up beforehand and need not be fancy. Each set consists of eleven cards numbered from zero to ten. One set (held in the right hand) is for the whole number. The left-hand set is for the decimal number. When a judge scores a performance, he or she holds up the appropriate cards so the emcee can read them. See the Judging and Scoring Rules on page 13 for details.

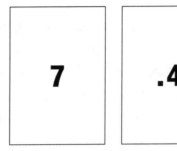

5. **Score keeper.** One person must be the official score keeper. This person writes down the names of the performers on a score sheet in the order in which they will perform. He or she writes the scores on the sheet as they are announced by the emcee and adds them up to obtain the composite score for each performer for that round. (See pages 16–17 for a sample score sheet.) A calculator is advisable to make sure scores are accurate. If there are enough volunteers, two people can act as score keepers: one to add and record the scores, and one to write them on a large board the audience can see.

6. **A time keeper.** This person times each contestant's performance to make sure the three-minute limit is not exceeded. If a contestant goes more than ten seconds over the three-minute limit, half of a point is deducted for every ten seconds thereafter. The time keeper must have an accurate timing device, such as a stop watch or digital timer. The timing device ideally should produce a sound at the three-minute mark so the performer and audience know the limit has been reached. The time keeper will inform the emcee if overtime points should be deducted.

7. **The audience.** They are there to enjoy the competition and encourage the poets to do their best. The audience should respect the performers by keeping silent during the performance. However, some slams allow some audience response of pleasure and displeasure during the performance. It will be up to the emcee to instruct the audience and to keep them under control. At the end of a performance the audience may be very demonstrative in order to influence the judges.

8. **The sacrificial poet.** Also known as the "Calibration Poet." In order to give the judges a chance to warm up and make sure they

understand what they are supposed to do, a poet who is not competing will perform the first poem and will be graded by the judges just as if he or she is in the competition. This will also decrease the negative psychological effect on the first poet in the official competition.

9. **Slammers.** A slam competition should have a minimum of three competing poets to make it really interesting. About fifteen poets is the maximum that can compete in a four-hour program. This assumes half an hour to prep the judges and audience, five minutes per poet per round, ten minutes between rounds, possible tie-off, and awarding of prizes. Each competitor should have at least four poems ready for the competition because there will usually be three rounds and possibly a tie-off. More will be said about the competitors under the Rules of the Slam and Performance Tips sections.

[THE RULES OF THE SLAM]

The following rules are based on the official rules of Poetry Slam, Inc., the National Poetry Slam organization. The complete rules can be found at www.poetryslam.com.

I. GENERAL PERFORMANCE RULES

Slam competitors must abide by the following rules in order not to be penalized or disqualified:

1. Poems can be on any subject and in any style, but only one poem may be performed during a poet's turn.
2. Each poet must perform only work that he or she has created.
3. No props (this is a complex and imprecise rule, subject to interpretation by the emcee). Generally, poets are allowed to use their given environment and the accoutrements it offers—microphones, mic stands, the stage itself—as long as these accoutrements are available to other competitors as well. However, musical instruments, prerecorded music, costumes, or other objects of any kind may **not** be used or introduced into a performance.
4. Sampling. It is acceptable for a poet to incorporate, imitate, or otherwise "signify on" the words, lyrics,

or tune of someone else in his own work. Or, as Poetry SIam, Inc., executive director Scott Marsh puts it, "The poet may 'riff off' another person's creative work, but may not 'rip off' that work."

5. The no-repeat rule. A poem may be used only once during the various rounds of the same competition.

6. The three-minute rule. Each competitor will have a maximum of three minutes and ten seconds to present a poem. Timing begins with the first intentional noise or gesture the poet makes. If the poet thinks there may be confusion as to when he or she begins, he or she should clue in the time keeper beforehand. The time keeper will alert the performer (without interrupting him or her) when three minutes are up. The performer then has ten seconds to complete the poem without a point deduction. A half point will be deducted for each ten seconds the performance continues beyond the three-minute, ten-second limit. However, the judges should **not** take going overtime into account in their judging.

8. The performer may interact verbally and even physically with the audience as long as the no props rule is not violated.

9. Violation of any of the above rules as determined by the emcee could result in disqualification or deduction of points.

II. TEAM PERFORMANCE RULES

1. Duos, trios, and quartets (otherwise known as team, group, or collaborative pieces) are allowed as long as all of the primary authors perform them.
2. The same rules govern performance by teams as by individuals.
3. A group may not perform a poem that is also performed by an individual during the same competition. (Some slam competitions are strictly for individuals, some are just for teams, others mix the two. The national championship is a mixed competition.)

III. JUDGING AND SCORING RULES

1. Each of the five judges will be selected by the emcee from among the audience members. The emcee will do his or her best to select fair and impartial judges.
2. Each judge will receive a page of written rules (see Appendix A on page 27) and will be briefly instructed in them by the emcee.
3. A judge may not be challenged over a score.
4. Each judge will score each poem from 0.0 to 10, with 10 being the highest possible score. Decimal places should be used to make ties more difficult.

Thus, each poem will receive five scores, one from each judge. The high and low scores will be eliminated and the middle three will be added together by the score keeper. The resulting total will constitute the score for that poet in that round. Scores in each round are added to the poet's score of previous rounds to produce a cumulative score. The highest possible score in each round is 30 (10 + 10 + 10), and the highest cumulative score for three rounds is 90 (30 + 30 + 30).

5. Reducing the field: The first round is complete when all competitors have performed their first poem and have been scored by the judges. At this point, the emcee eliminates the lowest-scoring third of the competitors (five, in the case of fifteen competitors). The remaining poets can continue in the same order or a new order can be selected after each round. At the end of the second round, the bottom half is eliminated, leaving the top five scoring poets to compete in the third round. At the end of the third round, the competitor with the highest combined score from all three rounds is the winner.

6. Ties: If, after three rounds, two or more poets have the same score, there will be a tie-off round. Performance order for this round will be determined by the flip of a coin or other method

of random selection. The poets will continue rounds of competition until a winning score is obtained by one poet.

7. Prizes: There is usually a grand prize for the overall winner and lesser prizes for second and third place. Often all competitors are given some sort of prize just for having the courage to compete. It is also a frequent practice to pass the hat among the audience to take up a monetary collection to be divided equally among nonwinners.

Although winning prizes is nice, the primary satisfaction to be gained is being able to effectively present poetry to an audience and have it be appreciated by them. Although a poetry slam is a competition, there is a distinct camaraderie among the poets. They enjoy each other's poetry and the energy and excitement they generate.

Poet	Scoring	Round 1	Round 2	S
Poet 1				
	Score A			
	Score B			
	Score C			
	Score D			
	Score E			
	Total of middle three			
	Time deduction			
	Note			
Poet 2				
	Score A			
	Score B			
	Score C			
	Score D			
	Score E			
	Total of middle three			
	Time deduction			
	Note			
Poet 3				
	Score A			
	Score B			
	Score C			
	Score D			
	Score E			
	Total of middle three			
	Time deduction			
	Note			

t R1+2	Round 3	Total R1+2+3	Tie Off Score

[PERFORMANCE STRATEGY]

Poetry slam competition would seem to be very simple and straightforward from the previous description of the proceedings. However, there are some strategic considerations.

Should a competitor do his or her best poem in the first round in order to have the best chance of making it to the second round? Or should he or she simply do a good-enough poem to probably get into the second round and save the better poems for the later rounds?

Deciding what poem to do in what round is perhaps the most important decision a competitor will make. Often this decision should be delayed until a few moments before performance so as to have the most information on which to base the decision.

The decision will depend on where the poet is in the performing schedule, what he or she knows or learns from the other competitors as they do their poems and receive their scores, and how the judges seem to be scoring. Do they like serious or lighter poems? Do they give higher scores for poetic content or for performance?

It is very important for a competitor to watch the performances of the other poets and to observe how they are scored by the judges.

[PERFORMANCE TIPS]

Each poet and poem is unique. That diversity is part of what makes slams so interesting. But there are some performance practices that enhance any performance.

First, speak as clearly and distinctly as possible without seeming unnatural so the audience and judges can easily hear the words of the poem. Many novice slammers mumble or slur their words, don't enunciate distinctly, or simply don't project their voices with enough volume. Even when a microphone is available, the poet often cannot be heard because he or she holds it too far from the mouth, or too close, causing distortion. Be sure to practice with the microphone before the actual performance if possible. Remember every microphone is different, more or less sensitive and more or less natural sounding.

A related matter is the delivery speed of the poem. Many slam poets try to impress with how rapidly they can perform their poems. Sheer speed can be impressive and can add to the excitement of the poem, but high velocity can also detract from a poem's effectiveness if it is difficult to understand or if the performer appears to be trying to cram as many words into his or her three minutes as possible. On the other hand, a poem done too slowly can be boring, especially if it has much repetition in it. The audience already knows what's coming.

The best practice is to vary the pace of performance to keep it interesting. Slow down to make a point or let the audience think about an idea

TRY TO CREATE AN IMMEDIATE POSITIVE IMPACT WITH THE BEGINNING OF YOUR PERFORMANCE. YOU ONLY HAVE ONE CHANCE TO MAKE A GOOD FIRST IMPRESSION.

and speed up to increase excitement and intensity. But always make sure the audience can hear and understand.

When you first come on the stage to do your poem, remember the rule that your time starts as soon as you connect with the audience. So make sure not to speak or motion to the audience until you are ready to begin. Try to create an immediate positive impact with the beginning of your performance. You only have one chance to make a good first impression.

If you can look into the eyes of the audience as you perform, it enhances your connection with them. But many poets find this too distracting. If so, gaze just over their heads at the back of the room most of the time. This gives the impression of looking at the audience.

Use your voice and body to effectively communicate the emotion inherent in the poem. Nothing will kill a slam performance faster than just reading or reciting a poem flatly, with no emotion in the voice. The performer must find and project to the audience the pathos, humor, dignity, innocence, power, beauty, disgust, wonder, or zaniness that the poem means to convey. Delivering the emotional intensity of the poem is the key to slam success.

For some reason, many slammers seem to think that just because they are allowed three minutes, they must take the whole time. Certainly the poem must last long enough to give the audience a distinct (and hopefully favorable) impression. Too short a poem may seem trivial despite the fact that some of our most honored poems are rather short. A slam is a performance, and the audience expects more than just a tidbit. But don't push the three-minute limit just because it's there. Make your poem its natural, most effective, length, and no longer.

Also, regarding the performance time: Clock your poems in practice so you know you can complete them well within the three-minute limit without strain.

Most slam performances are enhanced by appropriate use of the body. This is really what differentiates a slam performance from a poetry reading. At a reading the poet merely sits or stands, and the audience concentrates strictly on the meaning of the poem. The reader uses vocal emotion but seldom body animation. But slam requires the judges to base their score equally on the quality of the poem and the poet's performance.

The most successful slammers are good actors as

THE MOST SUCCESSFUL SLAMMERS ARE GOOD ACTORS AS WELL AS GOOD POETS. . . . AS MUCH CREATIVITY SHOULD BE PUT INTO FACIAL EXPRESSIONS AND BODY MOVEMENTS AS IS PUT INTO THE WORDS OF THE POEM ITSELF.

well as good poets. They are able to help the audience visualize what the poem describes. As much creativity should be put into facial expressions and body movements as is put into the words of the poem itself. Almost anything is allowed in the way of physical expression, so the poet should be as creative and daring as possible without violating the performance rules.

Still, the slammer should realize that some gestures or bodily movements, even if permissible, may be very effective in turning the judges **off**. Furthermore, some slams (particularly teen slams) are subject to school codes of conduct and language and may penalize or disqualify a performer for obscene, crude, or disrespectful language and gestures. The poet must carefully decide whether daring gestures or movements will enhance or detract from the presentation of his or her poem with each particular audience and group of judges.

Slams do not require competitors to perform their poems from memory. They may read the poem from a book or sheet of paper. However, this almost always puts the poet at a competitive disadvantage because it inhibits his or her ability to perform the poem. Also, the judges naturally feel that the poet who reads is less prepared than the one who recites. Sometimes, a poem must be read if the poet is in a tie-off and has run out of prepared performance poems. It's better to carry a copy of the poem if there is any doubt about having a poem completely memorized. If a memory lapse occurs during a performance, the poet may continue by referring to or reading from the written poem to the extent necessary. Do not use the book or paper in any way that would make it a prop, however.

Many slam poets have found that the body movements of the performance aid memorization of the words. The brain more easily remembers a particular physical movement than a word or phrase. Muscle memory causes and then reinforces recall of the associated words. So the best way to memorize and present a poem is to associate a particular physical gesture or expression with each phrase of the poem. But make the movements as natural and as appropriate to the words of the poem as possible. As with most difficult but worthwhile endeavors, practice perfects.

Concerning clothing, remember not to wear anything that could be construed as a costume. Moreover, don't wear clothing that will focus attention on it rather than on the poetry and the performance. For instance, don't wear a t-shirt with a message or picture that might draw attention. Slams are informal. Dress casually and keep it comfortable. Practice in clothing the same as or similar to what you will perform in.

The best way to learn how to slam successfully is to watch a slam performed by expert slammers. Observe how they speak and gesture. Listen to the emotional variety and power they give their words. Try to analyze their strengths and weaknesses. See if your evaluation of their performance agrees with that of the judges.

Finally, participate in slams as much as possible to perfect your craft. No matter how you score in a slam, take enjoyment from the performance and appreciation of your poetry. That's the whole point of slamming.

Remember to:

- Speak clearly and distinctly.
- Use good microphone technique.
- Put appropriate emotion into your spoken words.
- Vary the velocity of the poem.
- Use the amount of time that's right for the poem within the three-minute limit.
- Don't connect with the audience until you are ready to make a powerful beginning for your performance.
- Use gesture and movement creatively but carefully.
- Memorize the poem if possible.
- Use muscle memory to aid word memory.
- Wear and practice in casual, comfortable clothing.
- Observe and analyze performances by the best slammers.
- Participate in slams to become your best.
- Enjoy!

[WHAT MAKES A GOOD SLAM POEM?]

Good slam poems are usually different in several ways from good poems written to be read silently or in a regular poetry reading.

Slam poems are meant to be performed. Seen on the page, they may look simple and less interesting than when performed. They need performance in order to shine.

There is much good poetry that is dense with meaning, multilayered, deliberately ambiguous or confusing, and intellectually challenging. These elements do not usually make good slam poetry. Successful slam poetry must immediately, meaningfully, and emotionally connect with an audience. A good slam poem is fairly simple in structure, with content that is easily understood by someone hearing it for the first time.

A slam poem should be colorful and emotional, employ surprising or unusual but vivid images, and lend itself to performance with words that can be gestured or enhanced with body movement.

The best way to learn how to create good slam poems is to attend slams and observe slammers in action. To learn more about poetry slams, explore the resources listed in appendix B on page 29.

[APPENDIX A]

DIRECTIONS FOR JUDGES

The following is provided with permission from Poetry Slam, Inc., from www.poetryslam.com:

So You've Been Chosen to Judge a Poetry Slam
(An example of the written instructions for judges)

You have been enlisted in the service of poetry. This is supposed to be fun, and we don't expect you to be an expert, but we can offer certain guidelines that might help to make this more fun for everyone involved, especially you.

We use the word "poem" to include text and performance. Some say you should assign a certain number of points for a poem's literary merit and a certain number of points for the poet's performance. Others feel that you are experiencing the poem only through the performance, and it may be impossible to separate the two. Give each poem only one score.

- Trust your gut; and give the better poem the better score.
- Be fair. We all have our personal prejudices, but try to suspend yours for the duration of the slam. On the other hand, it's okay to have a prejudice

that favors the true and the beautiful over the mundane and superficial, the fascinating and enchanting over the boring and pedestrian.

- It's hard not to be influenced by the audience, but remember that in a quiet poem, the audience has no way to communicate what they're experiencing.
- The audience may boo you, that's their prerogative; as long as the better poem gets the better score, you're doing your job well.
- Be consistent with yourself. If you give the first poem a seven and the other judges give it a nine, that doesn't mean you should give the second poem a nine—unless it's a lot better than the first poem. In fact, if it's not as good as the first poem, we count on you to give it a lower score.
- Although the high and low scores will be thrown out, don't ever make a joke out of your score thinking that it doesn't really matter.
- Your scores may rise as the night progresses. That's called "Score Creep." As long as you stay consistent, you're doing your job well.
- The poets have worked hard to get here; treat them with respect. They are the show, not you (although there could be no show without you). All of us thank you for having the courage to put your opinions on the line.

[APPENDIX B]

ADDITIONAL SLAM RESOURCES

BOOKS

Poetry Slam, The Competitive Art of Performance Poetry,
edited by Gary Mex Glazner (Manic D Press, 2000),
237p., $15.
Includes a more complete discussion of slam
history, techniques, and personalities than could be
done in this manual. This is the next step for the
serious slammer.

Slam, edited by Cecily Von Ziegesar (Alloy Books,
2000), 160p., $5.99.
Provides poems and quotes from many slam and
traditional poets as well as some information about
slam competition.

*The Spoken Word Revolution: Slam, Hip Hop, and the
Poetry of a New Generation,* edited by Mark Eleveld
(Sourcebooks, 2003), 256p., $24.50.
Includes a CD of poetry by various slam and non-
slam poets narrated by Marc "Slam Pappy" Smith.

VIDEO

SlamNation, by Paul Devlin (1998), VHS, $29.95.
Excellent full-length documentary film about the

1998 National Poetry Slam finals in Seattle, Washington. Includes interviews and performances.

WEB SITE

www.poetryslam.com

This is the Web site of Poetry Slam, Inc., the official national poetry slam organization. It contains extensive information on rules and terminology, venues, schedules of events, photos of slammers, products for sale, opportunities to chat, and links to other slam sites.

[APPENDIX C]

CHECKLIST OF WHAT YOU'LL NEED

THINGS

- ❏ Room with chairs
- ❏ Stage or podium
- ❏ Microphone and sound system
- ❏ Container for names
- ❏ Timer/stop watch
- ❏ Bell or buzzer
- ❏ Scorecard sets
- ❏ Copies of rules for judges
- ❏ Calculator
- ❏ Easel, chalkboard,
  or posterboard to record scores

PEOPLE

- ❏ Emcee (master of ceremonies)
- ❏ Judges (three to five)
- ❏ Score keeper (two if possible)
- ❏ Time keeper
- ❏ Sacrificial poet
- ❏ Slammers (poets)
- ❏ Audience

[ABOUT THE AUTHOR]

Michael Baldwin, MLS, MPA, is director of the Benbrook (Tex.) Public Library. He is the author of two poetry chapbooks: *Why Is the Speed of Light So Slow?* And *Les Fleurs de L'Amour* (*Flowers of Love*). He also edited an anthology of poetry against child abuse, *What Child Is This?* Mr. Baldwin has been published extensively in poetry journals and has been a juried poet of the Houston Poetry Festival. He has participated in numerous poetry slams in Texas, and he cofounded the annual Bluebonnet Poetry Slam in Conroe, Texas.